I0170293

LYING
DEVIL

LYING DEVIL

Copyright © 2018 Randolph W. Mack. All rights reserved.

All rights reserved. No part of this publication may be reproduced, stored in a retrieval system, or transmitted in any way by any means – electronic, mechanical, photocopy, recording, or otherwise – without the prior permissions of the copyright holder, except by reviewer who may quote brief passages in a review to be printed in magazine newspaper or by radio / TV announcement, as provided by USA copyright law. The author and the publisher will not be held responsible for any errors within the manuscript. All characters appearing in this work are fictitious. Any resemblance to real persons, living or dead, is purely coincidental. Unless otherwise indicated, all scripture quotations are taken from the King James Version of the Bible.

FIRST EDITION

Published in 2019

Author: Randolph W. Mack

Website: www.RWMack.com

ISBN: 978-1-7337299-3-2

Library of Congress Control Number: TXu2-105-136 | July 5, 2018

Category: Religion

Library of Congress Cataloging-in-Publication Data

Editor: Barbara Joe (Amani Publishing LLC)

Proofreader: Kiera J. Northington (itsthewritestuff.com)

Photographer: Eric Bennett

Cover Designer: Barbara Upshaw-Mayers (Aura Graphics and Design)

Publishing Consultant & Formatting: Eli Blyden | EliTheBookGuy.com

Printed & Published in the United States of America

DEDICATION

To my three sons Shiloh Israel Mack, Adonis Israel Mack and Giavonnie Cartel Mack. I love you with all that I am and it is my true hope that you all will become the Men I did my best to inspire you to be. The world is yours, you just have to claim it! It's up to you to give 100 percent effort to be all you can and everything you want. Go get everything you want and stay away from everything you do not need. Always acknowledge God and He will never leave you or forsake you. Be strong in the Lord and in the power of His Might! Stick together and always be there for each other. Remember we all we got! Can't stop won't stop!

Love Always

Dad

Praise Yahweh

TABLE OF CONTENTS

LYING DEVIL

RANDOLPH W. MACK

Lying Devil

INTRODUCTION

This book was written through faith and by the grace of God. It is a look into my studies of the Scriptures and how I interpreted them.

The result of my experiences and research has led me to the point of being absolute! I did not hear the word absolute from anywhere nor did I hear anyone use it to describe one's faith. As I was praying one day, I realized my faith in God was unwavering, and I was absolutely positive my Lord was real!

From living, I've also experienced enough to know that Satan is also a deceptive and deadly force.

I titled this book Lying Devil because it is important to be able to discern the truth from a lie, the light from dark, right from wrong, and most of all, God's will for us to have salvation and eternal life.

This book can be used as a tool to elevate one's knowledge as well as a guide to bring clarity and understanding of the Scriptures.

It is my true hope that the result of reading and studying this book will bring you to the point of being absolute! In this book, I have taken it upon myself to simplify some of the words so the message can be readily understood. Examples from the King James Version: Ye is used to say you; Thy is used to say your; Thou can mean you as well. Although there are some changes, God's words are clear, and the message remains the same.

CHAPTER 1

The Liar,

The Murderer, The Deceiver

---◆---

John 8:44-45: "You are of your father the devil, and the lusts of your father you will do. He was a murderer from the beginning and abode not in the truth because there is no truth in him. When he speaks a lie, he speaks of his own: for he is a liar and the father of it and because I tell you the truth, you don't believe me?"

What is the purpose of a lie? To cover the truth! From the beginning of the world until the end in Revelation's, Satan has been on a mission to lie, kill, and deceive us.

Genesis 3:4 says, "And the serpent said unto the woman, you shall not surely die." This is Satan's first act of deception in the Bible. As you can see, it happened in the beginning.

When he told Eve that she would not die, he knew she certainly would. But the death would be spiritual, not physical.

Satan's biggest goal is to get us to be defiant toward God and to question God's word on whether they are true. But Satan knows God's words are true.

Matthew 4:5-6 says, "Then the devil takes him up into the holy city and sits him on a pinnacle of the temple. And said unto him, if you be the Son of God, cast thyself down: for it is written, He shall give his angels charge concerning you and in their hands, they shall bear you up lest at any time you dash your foot against a stone."

The four important words in these Scripture are when Satan says, "For it is written." Here it's clear that Satan is still trying to get Jesus to be defiant to God. This can be seen in the following verse when Jesus mentions the written word as being the truth when he says in Matthew 4:7: "Jesus said unto him, it is written again, you shall not tempt the Lord your God."

Another passage to let us know Satan and his devils know the words of God are true is Matthew 8:29 when the demons spoke directly to Jesus and made the statement, "What have we to do with you, Jesus, you Son of God? Are you come to torment us before our time?" Here we can conclude even the devils know their time is limited based on God's word.

While Satan tries to deceive the whole world into believing there are many gods, and we have no need to submit our will to God, James 2:19 comments on this: "You believe that there is one God; you do well: the devils also believe, and tremble."

You have to remember Satan was in heaven along with God and actually got to see His glory. He knows God is real and Almighty. He knows his time is limited, and he knows the words of God are true. Even though Satan knows the truth, all he wants us to believe are his lies. Then he tries to go to God and accuse us of being sinners. Revelation 12:10 says, "And I heard a loud voice saying in heaven, Now is come salvation, and strength, and the kingdom of our God, and the power of his Christ: for the accuser of our brothers is cast down, which accused them before our God day and night."

I mentioned earlier about it being said that there is only one God. God says in Isaiah 44:6: "This says the Lord the King of Israel, and his redeemer the Lord of hosts; I am the first, and I am the last; and beside me, there is no God." In the verse before that, Isaiah 44:5 says, "I am the Lord, and there is none else, there is no God beside me: I girded you, though you have not known me."

When it comes to overcoming Satan and all of his devices, we must lean on our Lord to help us get past them. God will make Satan's tricks known to us if we trust in the Scriptures. Or as Corinthians 2:11 says, "Lest Satan should get advantage of us: for we are not ignorant of his devices." When we think of Satan's devices, we must realize it is not something that should be overlooked as being small. We should not be surprised by the extent to which he will go to fool us. In 2 Corinthians 11:14, it says, "And no marvel; for Satan himself is transformed into an angel of light."

Great advice is also given by James 4:7, where he says, "Submit yourselves therefore to God. Resist the devil, and he will flee from you."

As we draw closer to the truth about God versus Satan, we must understand that we need God to help us overcome him. We cannot go toe to toe with Satan alone, but with our Lord, all things are possible.

We cannot be deceived or divided by class, culture, or even color. We are all one people created by God. Acts 17:24-26 says, "God that made the world and all things therein, seeing that he is Lord of heaven and earth, dwells not in temples made with hands; Neither is worshipped with men's hands, as though he needed anything, seeing he gives to all life, and breath, and all things; And hath made of one blood all nations of men for to dwell on all the face of the earth, and has determined the times before appointed, and the bounds of their habitation."

One of the biggest tricks Satan uses on us is to make us think we are different. But the Apostles in Acts are clear; we are all of one blood.

In closing this chapter, I will leave you with the words of Paul from the book of Romans 12:21, where he says, "Be not overcome of evil but overcome evil with good!"

CHAPTER 2

From A Serpent to A Dragon

———◆———

Genesis 3:1 is the first mention of Satan being a serpent. Verse 1 says, "Now the serpent was more subtle than any beast of which the Lord God had made. And he said unto the woman, "Yes, has God said, you shall not eat of every tree of the garden?"

From the time Adam and Eve were created, the serpent tried to get them to sin and disobey the one law God had instructed them not to violate.

When we look at Job 1:6, we will notice the serpent is now referred to as Satan.

Verse 6 says, "Now there was a day when the sons of God came to present themselves before the Lord, and Satan came with them." If we continue to read the book of Job, we will see that Satan is constantly trying to get between God and us. Satan is basically telling God that he can get Job to cuss Him to his face if he stopped protecting him.

God called Job perfect and upright in 1:8. But Satan told God that Job only respected and obeyed Him because God had blessed him. But regardless of what happened to Job, he never lost his faith in God.

As we continue to read, we come to the book of Isaiah 14:12. Satan is now being called Lucifer.

Although his name is changing, his character is not. He is constantly being deceptive and deadly with his intentions. By the time we get to verse 13-14, Lucifer states, "I will ascend into heaven, I will exalt my throne above the stars of God: I will sit also upon the mount of the congregation, in the sides of the north. I will ascend above the heights of the clouds; I will be like the most high." By this point, it is clear the serpent, Satan; Lucifer wants to make himself equal to God.

If we continue to go forward to Ephesians 6:11, we see the name devil. Verse 11 says, "Put on the whole armor of God, that you may be able to stand against the wiles of the devil." Revelation, the last book of the Bible clarifies that the serpent, Satan, the devil, Lucifer, and the great dragon are the same. He starts out as a serpent in Genesis and ends up a great dragon by Revelation's. Revelation 12:9 says, "And the great dragon was cast out, that old serpent, called the devil and Satan, which deceives the whole world: he was cast out into the earth, and his angels were cast out with him."

As I stated before, if one pays attention to the Scriptures, it is evident the serpent gets progressively worse. Not only is this true with the serpent, but people can likewise do as explained in Matthew 12:43-45: "When the unclean spirit is gone out of a man, he walks through dry places, seeking rest, and finds none. Then he says, I will return into my house from where I came out; and when he is come, he finds it empty, swept, and garnished. Then he goes and takes with himself seven other spirits more wicked than himself, and they enter in and dwell there: and the last state of that man is worse than the first."

I have seen this happen to a relative who recovered from drug abuse. He had successfully gone through rehab, gotten a good job, settled down, and then gotten married. He stayed on the straight and narrow for a few years, but soon he started drinking and smoking again. Before long, he was back to using hardcore drugs. Only this time, he was using every drug he could get his hands on. He was in and out of jail and became abusive to his family.

The point is, as the Scripture says in Matthew: A man can become worse than he was before without God in his life. When a person opens the door for Satan to come into his life, one can believe he will come in. This does not mean we have to be doing wrong when I say *open the door*. But we cannot assume because we are not doing anything wrong, that it means we're doing what's right.

It's not enough to say, "Well, I don't sell drugs, but I'm committing adultery." We can't say we're saved because we've never committed a murder, but we're involved in fornication. Neither is it acceptable to think just because we say we believe in God, that it is enough to keep us from being attacked by Satan.

We must follow the message of God that was spoken by James in 1:22, which says, "But be you doers of the word, and not hearers only, deceiving your own selves."

I've heard people say that to get to heaven we have to go through hell. From personal experience, I can say when it comes to accepting God, it seems like everything goes wrong all at the same time. At these times, we must stand firm in our faith in God and His words and trust that, as with Job, all things will be put back in place the right place.

In 1 Corinthians, it is encouraging when Paul says in 4:16-18: "For which cause we faint not; but though our outward man perish, yet the inward man is renewed day by day. For our light affliction, which is but for a moment, works for us a far more exceeding and eternal weight of glory; While we look not at the things which are seen, but at the things which are not seen: for the things which are seen are temporal; but the things which are not seen are eternal."

No matter how hard things seem to get, just press forward. Don't worry about material things or trivial gains. Focus on what's eternal and true.

In closing, remember 2 Corinthians 12:9-10 which says, "And he said unto me, 'My grace is sufficient for you: for my strength is made perfect in weakness.' Most gladly, therefore, will I rather glory in my infirmities, that the power of Christ may rest upon me. Therefore, I take pleasure in infirmities, in reproaches, in necessities, in persecutions, in distresses for Christ's sake: for when I am weak, then am I strong!"

Be strong in the Lord and the power of His might!

Lying Devil

CHAPTER 3

Roaring Lion
Seeking to Devour

❖

"**B**e sober, be vigilant, because your adversary the devil walks about like a roaring lion, seeking whom he may devour." In 1 Peter 5:8, Peter sheds light on how the devil walks about looking for people to destroy. Peter chose some strong language in describing the devil as a roaring lion. As I think of that, an image of a roaring lion comes to mind. Peter also uses the word devour. If one has ever seen a lion eating, then one knows it is a fearful sight. Putting that into the context of what Satan wants to do to us is even more fearful.

Notice that I used the name Satan in the last sentence of the paragraph above instead of the devil. I did that to remind us that he has more than one name. Not only that; many devils are just as mean and destructive as he is.

Mark 5:2-9 tells the story of a man with an unclean spirit living in him. In these verses, we can see there are many bad spirits. Verse 2 begins by saying, "And when he was come out of the ship, immediately there met him out of the tombs a man with an unclean spirit, who had his dwelling among the tombs; and no man could bind him, no, not with chains: Because that he had been often bound with fetters and chains, and the chains had been plucked asunder by him, and the fetters broken in pieces: neither could any man tame him. And always, night and day, he was in the mountains, and in the tombs, crying, and cutting himself with stones. But when he saw Jesus afar off, he ran and worshipped him, and cried with a loud voice, and said, What have I to do with you, Jesus, you the son of God? I adjure you by God, that you torment me not. For he said unto him, come out of the man, thou unclean spirit. And he asked him, what is your name? And he answered, saying, my name is Legion: for we are many."

What must not be overlooked is that this bad spirit identified itself by name and said that they were many. As I read that Scripture, I thought of the many times I've heard people speak, and it was like every other word was a cuss word. I've also heard some people speak in such a way, that although they were merely talking about being violent, the language seemed violent. Putting this together, I can't help but wonder when I've heard people speak like this if there were actually spirits speaking from within them. In saying that, it causes me to look back at my own life and shutter when I remember times I have spoken in ways that were less than pleasant. I'm sure some of us have had someone say something unpleasant, and then turned and said, "I'm sorry; I didn't mean that," as soon as it was out. Satan is so deceptive and can make himself appear to be something or someone that he's not. In 2 Corinthians 11:14, it says, "And no marvel; for Satan himself is transformed into an angel of light." So when it comes to causing confusion, he is the chief!

Job 1:6-7 also tells us that Satan goes to and fro in the earth seeking people to devour.

Verse 6-7 says, "Now there was a day when the sons of God came to present themselves before the Lord and Satan came also among them. And the Lord said unto Satan, Where did you come from? Then Satan answered the Lord, and said, "From going back and forth in the earth, and from walking up and down in it."

When I speak of Satan, the devil, and his legion of demons, it's important to realize that we, on our own, are no match for Satan, and he should not be taken lightly. In fact, it could be pure dangerous for not only us but also for those around us. Ephesians 6:10-17 gives us a clue as to what we are up against and how we should deal with it. Verse 10 says, "Finally, my brothers, be strong in the Lord and in the power of his might. Put on the whole armor of God that you may be able to stand against the wiles of the devil. For we wrestle not against flesh and blood, but against principalities, against powers, against the rulers of the darkness of this world, against spiritual wickedness in high places. Wherefore take unto you the whole armor of God that you may be able to withstand in the evil day, and having done all, to stand. Stand therefore, having your loins girt about with truth, and having on the breastplate of righteousness; And your feet shod with the preparation of the gospel of peace; Above all, taking the shield of faith, wherewith you shall be able to quench all the fiery darts of the wicked. And take the helmet of salvation, and the sword of the spirit, which is the word of God."

Paul brought up an important point when he said that there is spiritual wickedness in high places. In knowing this, we must worship God in spirit; we must be aware that Satan exists in the spiritual world as well as the physical. John 4:24 clarifies this when he says, "God is a spirit: and they that worship him must worship him in spirit and truth."

The first step we must take is to recognize God's will as opposed to doing what we want to do. Secondly, we must do as James suggests in 4:7 which is to: "Submit yourselves therefore to God. Resist the devil, and he will flee from you."

Once we submit our choices to God, He will make it clear to us what His will is for us. I have tried many things to fill what I felt was a void in my life. I tried to fill it with women, money, drugs, and alcohol, and most of the time it was all those things at the same time. Regardless of what I've tried, nothing has completed me the way I am now that I have acknowledged God and put Him first in my love and life. God is the piece of my life's puzzle that has made my life complete.

I know Satan would still devour me if given a chance, but I press forward knowing my Lord is with me and is true to His word when He speaks through Matthew and says that He will be with me, And He has power over all and everything in heaven and earth. So I know I will be protected from the evil of Satan.

Matthew 28:18-20 says, "And Jesus came and spoke unto them, saying, All power is given unto me in heaven and in earth. Go you therefore, and teach all nations, baptizing them in the name of the Father, and of the Son, and of the Holy Ghost: Teaching them to observe all things whatsoever I have commanded you: and lo, I am with you always, even unto the end of the world. Amen."

Be of good cheer! Our Lord is with us!

Lying Devil

CHAPTER 4

Heaven vs. Hell

Can one imagine being in heaven and the things one would see? A place where even flowers sing praises to God all the time, a place where we can see angels with our eyes not just in our minds. A place where we can see waterfalls of gold, and sit, and talk with Moses, Abraham, Israel, and other prophets of old. A place where even when it rains, we never get wet by a drop because the halo over our heads make sure it stops. A place where rain is not needed for thirst, but so that it will produce a rainbow to remind us of God's promise to never again flood the earth. I can only imagine this will be a place like no other; this is a place I will be able to again see my mother, my father, and my brother.

Can one imagine sitting with God one on one, and Him pointing to Jesus saying, "This is the one who gave His life for you; my only begotten Son."

We will see Jesus sitting on His majestic throne with angels all around Him saying, "This is the Chosen One whom the sins of the world were placed on."

Imagine seeing the one who never committed any sin and endured being crucified to unite us with our Father again. Imagine the living God whose love for us never wavered; imagine seeing our Lord, our King, and our Savior. Imagine in heaven, there will be no sickness or bad health and no need for money because love will be our true wealth. Yes, I feel heaven will be a beautiful place, and I pray to my Lord that it is not only my fate but also His will. From now on in my life, I will do my best to do what's right. I hope to be forgiven of my sins and be acceptable in God's sight. I've come to believe the best way for me to do this is to let prayers be the keys to my days and faith the locks of my nights. So no matter how many times I rise or fall, to my Lord will I give my all and all. I hope everyone can see this vision of mine and that the stairway to heaven will be easy to find. So even if we are separated by space or time, I'll see everyone in paradise as long as we have one God, one faith, one love, and one mind.

I wrote that poem after reading Proverbs 15:24, which says, "The way of life is above to the wise that he may depart from hell beneath." After reading that Scripture, I started to think about what I imagined heaven would be like. I've heard people say that heaven is simply a pleasant state of mind, but the Scriptures are clear that heaven is a separate and distinct place from where we are now. I'm not sure how one can say they believe in God's words and conclude that heaven is simply a pleasant thought. If that was the case, then what was the purpose of Jesus being crucified? If it were that easy, wouldn't we all be in heaven all the time by just thinking it? Besides that, the entire Scripture and the faith are based on the life, death, and resurrection of Jesus and the promise of eternal life in heaven.

Many Scriptures show heaven and earth are two different places. John 14:1-2 says that heaven has many mansions. Verses 1 and 2 says, "Let not your heart be troubled: you believe in God, believe also in me. In my Father's house there are many mansions: if it were not so, I would have told you. I go to prepare a place for you."

Matthew 13:31-50 explains who will inherit the kingdom of heaven. Verse 31 starts by saying, "Another parable put he forth unto them, saying, The kingdom of heaven is like a grain of mustard seed, which a man took, and sowed in his field: which indeed is the least of all seeds: but when it is grown, it is the greatest among herbs, and becomes a tree, so that the birds of the air come and lodge in the branches thereof. Another parable spoke he unto them; The kingdom of heaven is like unto leaven which a woman took, and hid in three measures of meal, till the whole was leavened. All these things spoke Jesus unto the multitude in parables; and without a parable spoke he not unto them: That it might be fulfilled which was spoken by the prophet saying, I will open my mouth in parables; I will utter things which have been kept secret from the foundation of the world. Then Jesus sent the multitude away, and went into the house: and his disciples came unto him, saying, Declare unto us the parables of the tares of fields. He answered and said unto them, He that sows the good seed is the Son of man; The field is the world; the good seed are the children of the kingdom; but the tares are the children of the wicked one; The enemy that sowed them is the devil; the harvest is the end of the world; and the reapers are the angels. As therefore the tares are gathered and burned in the fire; so shall it be in the end of this world. The Son of man shall send forth his angels, and they shall gather out of his kingdom all things that offend, and them which do iniquity; And shall cast them into a furnace of fire: there shall be wailing and gnashing of teeth. Then shall the righteous shine forth as the sun in the kingdom of their Father. Who has ears to hear, let him hear. Again the kingdom of heaven is like unto treasure hid in a field; which when a man has found, he hides, and for joy thereof goes and sells all that he has, and buy that field. Again, the kingdom of heaven is like unto a merchant man, seeking goodly pearls: Who, when he had found one pearl of great price, went and sold all that he had, and bought it. Again, the kingdom of heaven is like unto a net that was cast into the sea, and gathered of every kind: Which, when it was full, they drew to shore, and sat down, and gathered the good into vessels, but cast the bad away. So shall it be at the end of the world: the angels shall come forth, and sever the wicked from among the just, And shall cast them into the furnace of fire: there shall be wailing and gnashing of teeth."

It is clear from reading the above Scriptures that God has a plan to separate the good from the bad. To say God's name and not do His will, will not be enough. Matthew 7:21 confirms this by saying, "Not everyone that says unto me, Lord, Lord, shall enter into the kingdom of heaven; but he that does the will of my Father which is in heaven."

Several Scriptures describe hell as being a place of torment. Matthew 25:41 says, "Then shall he say also to them on the left hand, Depart from me, you cursed, into everlasting fire prepared for the devil and his angels."

Isaiah 66:22-24 says, "For as the new heavens and the new earth, which I will make, shall remain before me, says the Lord, so shall your seed and your name remain. And it shall come to pass, that from one new moon to another and from one Sabbath to another, shall all flesh come to worship before me, says the Lord. And they shall go forth, and look upon the bodies of the men that have transgressed against me: for their worm shall not die, neither shall their fire be quenched; and they shall be an abhorring unto all flesh."

Revelation 14:10-11 says, "The same shall drink of the wine of the wrath of God, which is poured out without mixture into the cup of his indignation; and he shall be tormented with fire and brimstone in the presence of the holy angels, and in the presence of the Lamb: And the smoke of their torment ascends up for ever and ever: and they have no rest day or night who worship the beast and his image, and whosoever receives the mark of his name."

Revelation 19-20 says, "And the beast was taken, and with him the false prophets that wrought miracles before him, with which he deceived them that worshipped his image. These both were cast alive into a lake of fire and brimstone, where the beast and the false prophet are, and shall be tormented day and night for ever and ever."

I've heard it said many times, "Don't worry about or study the book of Revelation's." I don't know how that got started, but I question how one can feel a book is understood and not know what the end is.

In 2 Timothy 2:15, we are advised to study. He says, "Study to show thyself approved unto God, a workman that need not to be ashamed, rightly dividing the word of truth."

All my life I have heard people talk about heaven and hell. In doing so, I have concluded that both are real. The decision we have to make to believe this is our own choice and ours alone. We will have to carry our own crosses. I have accepted God's word as being faithful and true, and with that, I have submitted my will, love, and life to Him so that I will have eternal life in heaven.

"For the time is come that judgment must begin at the house of God: and if it first begins at us, what shall the end be of them that obey not the gospel of God?" 1 Peter 4:17

CHAPTER 5

Riches

———◆———

"**F**or we brought nothing into this world, and it is certain we can carry nothing out. And having food and raiment let us be therewith content. But they that will be rich fall into temptation and a snare and into many foolish and hurtful lusts, which drown men in destruction and perdition. For the love of money is the root of all evil: which while some coveted after they have erred from the faith and pierced themselves through with many sorrows." I Timothy 6:7-10

I included riches to be part of this book because it is the basis of so many of our problems. It should be noted that Timothy said, "The love of money is the root of all evil." Not money, but the love of money! People all over the world will do many things to get money, but it's never enough. People will rob, steal, and even kill for money. But if they applied the Scriptures to their pursuit of money, maybe their willingness to make it the most important thing in their lives would change. Matthew 19:23-24 says, "Then said Jesus unto his disciples,

Verily I say unto you, it is easier for a camel to go through the eye of a needle, than for a rich man to enter into the kingdom of God."

I can remember the first time I read that Scripture. I thought of what the eye of a needle was shaped like and the size of it. Then I visualized the hump of a camel and the size of it. The first thought I had was that would be impossible! So the question I had was, "Does it mean it will be impossible for a rich man to go to heaven?"

In Luke 18:16-24, a man asked Jesus what will it take for him to inherit eternal life? Verse 16 says, "But Jesus called them unto him and said, 'Suffer little children to come unto me and forbid them not: for of such is the kingdom of God. Verily I say unto you, whosoever shall not receive the kingdom of God as a little child shall in no means enter therein. And a certain ruler asked him saying, Good Master, what shall I do to inherit eternal life? And Jesus said unto him, why call you me good? None is good, save one that is God. You know the commandments, do not commit adultery, do not kill, do not steal, do not bear false witness, honor thy father and thy mother. And he said, all these have I kept from my youth up. Now when Jesus heard these things, he said unto him, Yet lack you one thing: sell all that you have and distribute unto the poor and you will have treasure in heaven: and come, follow me. And when he heard this, he was very sorrowful: for he was very rich. And when Jesus saw that he was very sorrowful, he said, How hardly shall they that have riches enter into the kingdom of heaven?"

I can imagine how the man felt when it's said that he was sorrowful. Can we put ourselves in his position? Even with Jesus telling him to give away all of his possessions. His faith had to be unwavering, to say the least. The situation this man was put in was one we all are in. Maybe we are not all rich, but we all must make a choice to put God above and before anything, anyone, and everything.

Matthew 6:19-21 guides us in understanding where our values should be. Verse 19 says, "Lay not up for yourselves treasures upon earth, where moth and rust do corrupt, and where thieves do not break through and steal: for where your treasure is there will your heart be also!" From reading that, I can't help but say that it's true. I know people, even close family members, who treat their possessions, especially their homes, like it is heaven. The reason it may be easier for a camel to walk through the eye of a needle than for a rich man to inherit the kingdom of heaven is he thinks he has everything he needs, and he can buy everything he wants.

A lot of rich people are anti-social, arrogant, and rude. A lot of rich people are also the same when it comes to charity. They won't give anyone the dirt off a dime!

Saying that reminds me of the story of Lazarus and the rich man in the book of Luke 16:20-31, which says, "And there was a certain beggar named Lazarus, which was laid at his gate, full of sores, and desiring to be fed with the crumbs which fell from the rich man's table: moreover the dogs came and licked his sores. And it came to pass that the beggar died, and was carried by the angels into Abraham's bosom: the rich man also died and was buried; and in hell, he lifts up his eyes being in torments and sees Abraham afar off and Lazarus in his bosom. And he cried and said, Father Abraham, have mercy on me and send Lazarus that he may dip the tip of his finger in water and cool my tongue; for I am tormented in this flame. But Abraham said, Son, remember that you in your lifetime received thy good things and likewise Lazarus evil things: but now he is comforted, and you are tormented. And besides all this, between us and you there is a great gulf fixed: so that they which would pass from hence to you cannot; neither can they pass to us that would come from there. Then he said, I pray thee therefore, father, that you would send him to my father's house: For I have five brothers; that he may testify unto them, lest they also come into this place of torment. Abraham said unto him, They have Moses and the prophets; let them hear them. And he said, Nay, father Abraham: but if one went unto them from the dead, they will repent. And he said unto him, If they hear not Moses and the prophets, neither will they be persuaded, though one rose from the dead."

Understanding that Scripture reminds me to treat others the way I want to be treated regardless of how they look or what they have. The rich man had his heaven here on earth and probably looked down on Lazarus as if he was beneath him. However, when he passed, he wanted to use Lazarus to warn his brothers to change their ways before it was too late for them. Throughout the Bible, there are warnings about people who spend their lives chasing riches. Proverbs 11:4 says, "Riches profit not in the day of wrath: but righteousness delivers from death."

Proverbs 13:11 says, "Wealth gotten by vanity shall be diminished: but he that gathered by labor shall increase."

In 1 John 2:15-17, it goes further. He says, "Love not the world, neither the things that are in the world. If any man loves the world, the love of the Father is not in him. For all that is in the world, the lust of the flesh, and the lust of the eyes, and the pride of life, is not of the Father, but is of the world. And the world passes away, and the lust thereof: but he that will do the will of God abides for ever."

It's clear; we all live by chance, but it's even clearer that we all love by choice. We must be careful of the choices we make when it comes to doing what we want as opposed to doing God's will. One of my favorite Scriptures is in Proverbs 30:7-9. I pray this prayer and try to live my life by this standard. Verse 7 says, "Two things have I required of you; deny me not before I die: Remove far from me vanity and lies: give me neither poverty nor riches; feed me with food convenient for me: Lest I be full, and deny thee, and say, Who is the Lord? Or lest I be poor, and steal, and take the name of my God in vain."

In closing, I direct you to Proverbs 3:5-7, which says, "Trust in the Lord with all your heart; and lean not on your own understanding. In all your ways acknowledge him, and he shall direct your paths. Be not wise in your own eyes: fear the Lord and depart from evil."

Consider Me

Will you consider me, a man with goals and aspirations, to lead the children my Lord has entrusted me with back to Him? Also to be a loving husband to my wife and family as I put God first in my pursuit of His will for my life. Consider my ability to lead and set standards that others will follow. Consider that where I have been so far is only a prelude of where I have the potential to go.

I've heard it said that behind every dark cloud there is a silver lining. The silver lining for me is that I have developed the understanding to apply to the wisdom and knowledge I already had. From this, my ultimate mission in this life is to pursue eternal life in the one to come. Consider I understand being loyal is more than a belief; it's a way of life. Consider I understand the meaning of love and all it encompasses. Consider I am a man among men. I have been smooth as silk and as rough as concrete. I have been dangerous and protective. I have been free and in bonds. I have experienced poverty and wealth. (Lord, forgive my trespasses). My hands have embraced my children, and these same hands have punished men! I have sought after love only to be pursued by hate. I have experienced smiles as well as cries. I have witnessed death and the beginning of my son's life. Consider I have experienced much, and in taking all this into account, consider that when I tell you I have not experienced anything which compares to the love of God—I'm telling you the truth.

CHAPTER 6

God Is the Truth

Job 38:1-41 says, "Then the Lord answered Job out of the whirlwind, and said, Who is this that darkened counsel by words without knowledge? Gird up now your loins like a man: for I will demand of thee, and answer you me. Where were you when I laid the foundations of the earth? Declare, if you have understanding. Who has laid the measures thereof, if you know? Or who has stretched the line upon it? Whereupon are the foundations thereof fastened? Or who laid the corner stone thereof; When the morning stars sang together, and all the sons of God shouted for joy? Or who shut up the sea with doors, when it brake forth, as if it had issued out of the womb? When I made the cloud the garment thereof, and thick darkness a swaddling band for it, And break up for it my decreed place, and set bars and doors. And said, Here to shall you come, but no further: and here shall your proud waves be stayed? Have you commanded the morning since your days; and caused the dayspring to know his place; That it might take hold of the ends of the earth, that the wicked might be shaken out of it? It is turned as clay to the seal; and they stand as a garment. And from the wicked their light is withheld, and the high arm shall be broken. Have you entered into the springs of the sea? Or have you walked in the search of the depth? Have the gates of death been opened onto you? Or have you seen the doors of the shadow of death? Have you perceived the breadth of the earth? Declare if you know it all. Where is the way where light dwells? And as for darkness where is the place thereof. That you should take it to the bound thereof, and that you should know the paths to the house thereof? Know you it, because you were then born? Or because the number of your days is great? Have you entered into the treasures of the snow? Or have you seen the treasures of the hail, Which I have reserved against the time of trouble, against the day of battle and war? By what way is the light parted, which scatters the east wind upon the earth? Who has divided a watercourse for the overflowing of waters, or a way for the lightning of thunder; To cause it to rain on the earth, where no man is; on the wilderness, wherein there is no man; To satisfy the desolate and waste ground; and to cause the bud of the tender herb to spring forth? Have the rain a father? Or who has begotten the drops of dew? Out of whose womb came the ice? And the hoary frost of heaven, who has gendered it? The waters are hid as with a stone and the face of the deep is frozen. Can you bind the sweet influences of Pleiades, or loose the bands of Orion? Can you bring forth Mazzaroth in his season? Or can you guide Arcturus with his sons? Know you the ordinances of heaven? Can you set the dominion thereof in the earth? Can you lift up your voice to the clouds, that abundance of waters may cover you? Can you send lightning's that they may go, and say unto thee, Here we are? Who has put wisdom in the inward parts? Or who has given understanding to the heart? Who can number the clouds in wisdom? Or who can stay the bottles of heaven, when the dust grows into hardness, and the clods cleave fast together? Will you hunt the prey for the lions? When they couch in their dens, and abide in the covert to lie and wait? Who provides the raven his food? When his young ones cry unto God, they wander for lack of meat."

Job 39:1-30: "Know you the time when the wild goats of the rock bring forth? Or can you mark when the hinds do calf? Can you number the months that they fulfill? Or know the time they bring forth? They bow themselves, they bring forth their young ones, they cast out their sorrows. Their young ones are in good liking, they grow up with corn; they go forth, and return not unto them. Who has sent out the wild ass free? Or who has loosed the bands of the wild ass? Whose house I have made the wilderness, and the barren land his dwelling. He scorns the multitude of the city, neither regards he the crying of the driver. The range of the mountains is his pasture, and he searches after every green thing. Will the unicorn be willing to serve thee, or abide by thy crib? Can you bind the unicorn with his band in the furrow? Or will he harrow the valleys after you? Will you trust him, because his strength is great? Or will you leave your labor to him? Will you believe him, that he will bring home thy seed and gather it into thy barn? Gave you the goodly wings unto the peacocks? Or wings and feathers unto the ostrich? Which leaves her eggs in the dust, and forgets that the foot may crush them, or that the wild beast may break them. She is hardened against her young ones, as though they were not hers: her labor is in vain without fear; Because God has deprived her of wisdom, neither has he imparted to her understanding. What time she lifts up herself on high, she scorns the horse and the rider. Have you given the horse strength? Have you clothed his neck with thunder? Can you make him afraid as a grasshopper? The glory of his nostrils is terrible. He paws in the valley, and rejoices in his strength: he goes on to meet the armed men. He mocks at fear, and is not affrighted; neither turns he back from the sword. The quiver rattles against him, the glittering spear and the shield. He swallows the ground with fierceness and rage: neither believeth he that it is the sound of the trumpet. He says among the trumpets, ha, ha; and he smells the battle afar off, the thunder of the captains, and the shouting. Do the hawk fly by your wisdom, and stretch her wings towards the south? Do the eagle mount up at your command, and make her nest on high? She dwells and abides on the rock, upon the crag of the rock, and her eyes behold afar off. Her young ones also suck up blood: and where the slain are, there is she."

Job 40:1-24: "Moreover the Lord answered Job and said, Shall he who contends with the Almighty instruct him? He that reproved God, let him answer it. Then Job answered the Lord, and said, Behold, I am vile; what shall I answer you. I will lay my hand upon my mouth. Once I have spoken; but I will not answer: yea, twice; but I will proceed no further. Then answered the Lord unto Job out of the whirlwind, and said, Gird up your loins now like a man: I will demand of you, and declare you unto me. Will you condemn me, that you may be righteous? Have you an arm like God? Or can you thunder with a voice like him? Deck yourself now with majesty and excellence; and array yourself with glory and beauty. Cast abroad the rage of the wrath: and behold every one that is proud, and abase him. Look on every one that is proud, and bring him low; and tread down the wicked in their place. Hide them in the dust together; and bind their faces in secret. Then will I confess unto you that your own right hand can save you. Behold now behemoth, which I made with you; he eats grass as an ox. Lo now, his strength is in his loins, and his face is in the navel of his belly. He moves his tail like a cedar: the sinews of his stones are wrapped together. His bones are as strong pieces of brass; his bones are like bars of iron. He is the chief of the ways of God: he that made him can make his sword to approach unto him. Surely the mountain brings him forth food, where all the beasts of the field play. He lies under the shady trees, in the covert of reed, and fens, The shady trees cover him with their shadow; the willows of the brook compass him about. Behold, he drinks up a river, and has not: he trusts that he can draw up Jordan into his mouth. He takes it with his eyes: his nose pierces through snares."

I began this chapter with these verses to show the side of God He rarely shows. In these verses, we hear God speak about things from one extreme to another. In one verse, He speaks about how He created the world. Then in another verse, He speaks about supplying food for birds. Most of the time when God speaks in the Bible, He is so very humble and loving. Although He's still doing that in these verses, He speaks with authority to let it be known He is the true living God and the Creator of all things.

I have met so many people who reduced God to a level where they seem to think they can pick Him up and put Him down whenever they want. To those who do and take things for granted, I would advise them to remember Hebrews 10:31, which says, "It is a fearful thing to fall into the hands of the living God."

I titled this chapter "God Is The Truth" to get us to focus on the promises He has made to us concerning eternal life in heaven or hell. David made a comment that has stood out to me for years about God being omnipresent. Psalm 139:1-8 says, "O Lord, you have searched, and known me. You know my downsitting and mine uprising, you understand my thoughts afar off. You compassest my path and my lying down, and art acquainted with all my ways. For there is not a word in my tongue, but, lo, O Lord, you know it altogether. You have beset me behind and before, and laid your hand upon me. Such knowledge is too wonderful for me; it is high, I cannot attain unto it. Where shall I go from thy spirit? Or where shall I flee from your presence? If I ascend up into heaven, you art there: if I make my bed in hell, behold, you are there." When I read those verses, I can't help but feel the power of God. Paul, in 1 Corinthians 4:20, felt the same way when he said, "For the kingdom of God is not in word, but in power."

Our whole faith is based on our acceptance of the word of God and that it is the truth. Paul describes the word of God in Hebrews 4:12, where he says, "For the word of God is quick, and powerful, and sharper than any two-edged sword, piercing even to the dividing asunder of soul and spirit, and of joints and marrow, and is a discerner of the thoughts and intents of the heart."

When we worship God, we must do it from our hearts. John 4:23 confirms this when he says, "But the hour come, and now is, when the true worshippers shall worship the Father in spirit and in truth: for the Father seeks such to worship him." As long as I have been studying the Bible, and applying it to my life, I can say that God is the truth! Everything His word has said has come true in my life.

In closing, I want to direct attention to John 4:7-8, which says, "Beloved, let us love one another: for love is of God;

and every one that loves is born of God, and knows God. He that loves not knows not God; for God is love."

Lastly, James 1:22 says, "But be you doers of the word, and not hearers only, deceiving yourselves."

Go Forward

In this life, it is our destiny to go forward. In spite of our adversities, we must push ahead. Despite facing obstacles, we must strive to reach our goals. Having a desire to succeed must become more than a wish. In action, it must become a way of life. All of the things we set out to accomplish in life must be based in reality and be within our potential to reach them. With this, we should focus on the process of finishing rather than worrying about what could prevent us from being successful. In essence, we should see ourselves at the completion of our goals even as we focus on setting them.

In our lives, we will all face some trials. Some will be by chance and some through our choices. Being enlightened by them is the paths we traverse to become mature adults and distinguishers in the difference between what's good to us versus what's good for us. Even being able to discern the truth from a lie.

Regardless of what we set out to do, we must realize, as we go forward in life, what counts is not how fast we go but rather how far we get that matters. Going forward is an ability some inherit, and some will evolve into. Regardless of how it's acquired, the drive to hold on after others would let go is the same thing that separates challengers from champions. Going forward means letting go of hurt from others, not because we are weak, but because are strong. Strong enough to accept disappointments from others with the grace of an adult instead of with the grief of a child. Going forward motivates us to lead rather than follow.

Being a leader invokes others around us to also give their best and the rest to fulfill their destiny and purpose. So be a star and always remember to shine, knowing that your light could lead the way for others to go forward!

CHAPTER 7

Faith

———◇———

“Now faith is the substance of things hoped for, the evidence of things not seen. For by it, the elders obtained a good report. Through faith, we understand that the worlds were framed by the word of God, so things which are seen were not made of things which do appear. By faith Abel offered unto God a more excellent sacrifice than Cain, by which he obtained witness that was righteous, God testifying of his gifts: and by it, he being dead yet speaks. By faith Enoch was translated that he should not see death; and was not found, because God had translated him: for before his translation he had this testimony, that he pleased God. But without faith, it is impossible to please him: for he that comes to God must believe that he is, and that he is a rewarder of them that diligently seek him. By faith Noah, being warned of God of things not seen as yet, moved with fear, prepared an ark to the saving of his house; by the which he condemned the world, and became heir of the righteousness which is by faith. By faith Abraham, when he was called to go out into a place which he should after receive for an inheritance, obeyed; and he went out not knowing where he went. By faith he sojourned in the land of promise, as in a strange country, dwelling in tabernacles with Isaac and Jacob, the heirs with him of the same promise: For he looked for a city which hath foundations, whose builder and maker is God. Through faith also Sara herself received strength to conceive seed, and was delivered of a child when she was past age, because she judged him faithful who had promised. Therefore sprang there even of one, and him as good as dead, so many as the stars of the sky in multitude, and as the sand which is by the sea shore innumerable. These all died in faith, not having received the promises, but having seen them afar off, and were persuaded of them, and embraced them, and confessed and they were strangers and pilgrims on the earth. For they that say such things declare plainly that they seek a country. And truly, if they had been mindful of that country from where they came out, they might have had opportunity to have returned. But now they desire a better country, that is, a heavenly: wherefore God is not ashamed to be called their God: for he has prepared for them a city. By faith Abraham, when he was tried, offered up Isaac: and he that had received the promises offered up his only begotten son, Of whom it was said, That in Isaac shall your seed be called: Accounting that God was able to raise him up, even from the dead; from where also he received him in a figure. By faith Isaac blessed Jacob and Esau concerning things to come. By faith Jacob, when he was a dying, blessed both the sons of Joseph; and worshipped, leaning upon the top of his staff. By faith Joseph, when he died, made mention of the departing of the children of Israel; and gave commandment concerning his bones. By faith Moses, when he was born, was hidden three months of his parents, because they saw he was a proper child; and they were not afraid of the king's commandment. By faith Moses, when he was come to years, refused to be called the son of Pharaoh's daughter; choosing rather to suffer affliction with the people of God, than to enjoy the pleasures of sin for a season; Esteeming the reproach of Christ greater riches than the treasures in Egypt: for he had respect unto the recompense of the reward. By faith he forsook Egypt, not fearing the wrath of the king: for he endured, as seeing him who is invisible. Through faith he kept the Passover, and the sprinkling of the blood, lest he that destroyed the firstborn should touch them. By faith they passed through the red sea as by dry land: which the Egyptians assaying to do were drowned. By faith the walls of Jericho fell down, after they were compassed about seven days. By faith the harlot Rahab perished not with them that believed not, when she had received the spies with peace. And what shall I more say? For the time would fail me to tell of Gideon, and of Barak, and of Samson, and of Jephthah;

of David also, and Samuel and of the prophets: who through faith subdued kingdoms, wrought righteousness, obtained promises, stopped the mouths of lions. Quenched the violence of fire, escaped the edge of the sword, out of weakness were made strong, waxed valiant in fight, turned to flight the armies of the aliens. Women received their dead raised to life again: and others were tortured, not accepting deliverance; that they might obtain a better resurrection. And others had trial of cruel mockings and scourging, yea, moreover of bonds and imprisonment: They were stoned, they were sawn asunder, were tempted, were slain with the sword: they wandered about in sheepskins and goatskins; being destitute, afflicted, tormented; Of whom the world was not worthy: they wandered in deserts, and in mountains, and in dens and caves of the earth. And these all, having obtained a good report through faith, received not the promise: God having provided some better thing for us, that they without us should not be made perfect." Hebrews 11:1-40

Of all the chapters in this book, this is by far the most important one. Having faith in God's words as being true is what our whole religion is based on. I began this chapter with examples of how faith has been the cornerstone of so many distinguished people in the Bible. Faith has helped some begin life as well as prevent death to others. By faith, I even wrote this book. Many of the prophets spoke of faith throughout the Bible, and if we look into any religions, they are based on faith to some extent or extreme. Even in our most adverse times, we must continue to have faith. Hebrews 10:23 says, "Let us hold fast the profession of our faith without wavering; (for he is faithful that promised)."

In my life, I have been in situations where I felt there was no way I would emerge to the other side of them. That was on my own, but through my faith in God's word, I let go and let God! I had to get to the point where even though it seemed like God was not hearing me or refused to answer, in fact, He did. If I asked for something, and He did not give it to me, it probably was not meant for me to have it according to His will. I had to grow to the point where I would say, "Well, if God did not give me what I asked for, then it's probably something I could not see that would be harmful." Having faith that my Lord is with me means I believe I will be protected by things seen and unseen. God knows I've learned everything that's good to me is not good for me. That applies to people as well!

So even when things may not go the way we want or in the time we want, we must stand firm and continue to believe in the Scriptures. In James, he gives us some direction to accomplish this. Verse 1:2-8 says, "My brethren, count it all joy when you fall into divers temptations; knowing this, that the trying of your faith works patience but let patience have her perfect work, that you may be perfect and entire, wanting nothing. If any of you lack wisdom, let him ask of God, that gives to all men liberally and upbraideth not; and it shall be given him, but let him ask in faith, nothing wavering. For he that wavers is like a wave of the sea driven with the wind and tossed. For let not that man think that he shall receive anything of the Lord. A double minded man is unstable in all ways."

Now it's one thing to have faith, but faith must be shown through our works. As James 2:26 says, "For as the body without the spirit is dead, so faith without works is dead also." Let me go back before I go forward and let James explain what faith and works are. James says in

2:14-18, "What does it profit, my brethren, if a man says he has faith but does not have works? Can faith save him? If a brother or sister be naked and destitute of daily food and one of you say unto them, Depart in peace, be you warmed and filled; not withstanding you give them not those things which are needful to the body; what does it profit? Even so faith if it has not works, is dead, being alone. Yea, a man may say, you have faith and I have works: show me your faith without your works and I will show you by my works."

When it comes to works, we must all put on the spirit of charity and humble ourselves. But to get the kind of faith mentioned in the Scriptures, we have to be willing to be tested on different levels to reinforce it. In I Peter 1:6-10, Peter encourages us to hold on in spite of adversity while trying to solidify our faith. Verse 6 says, "Wherein you greatly rejoice, though now for a season, if need be you are in heaviness through manifold temptations: That the trial of your faith, being much more precious than of gold that perishes though it be tried with fire, might be found unto praise and honor and glory at the appearing of Jesus Christ: Who having not seen, you love; in who, though now you see him not, yet believing, you rejoice with joy unspeakable and full of glory: Receiving the end of your faith, even the salvation of your souls. Of which salvation the prophets have inquired and searched diligently, who prophesied of the grace that should come unto you."

As I said earlier, there are many Scriptures to encourage us to have faith and, in some instances, we are encouraged to even fight for it. In 1Timothy 6:12, he says, "Fight the good fight of faith, lay hold on eternal life, where unto you are also called, and have professed a good profession before many witnesses." And it goes on through the Bible.

Romans 5:1-2 says, "Therefore being justified by faith, we have peace with God through our Lord Jesus Christ. By whom also we have access by faith into this grace wherein we stand, and rejoice in hope of the glory of God."

Romans 10:17 says, "So faith comes by hearing and hearing by the word of God."

In 2 Corinthians 5:7, it says, "For we walk by faith, not by sight."

Ephesians 2:8 says, "For by grace are you saved through faith; and that not of yourselves: it is the gift of God."

Matthew 17:20 says, "And Jesus said unto them, Because of your unbelief; for verily I say unto you if you have faith as a grain of mustard seed, you shall say unto this mountain, remove from here to over there; and it shall remove; and nothing shall be impossible unto you."

Matthew 25:21 says, "His lord said unto him, Well done, thou good and faithful servant: you have been faithful over a few things, I will make you ruler over many things: enter you into the joy of the Lord."

It can be seen that faith is an essential component of believing in God's words. I can remember hearing the saying, "Stand for something, so you don't keep falling for anything!"

From the moment I opened my heart to God and trusted Him to guide my choices, my life has become clearer as to what my purpose is according to His will. In everything I do, I include my Lord in it to make certain it is in line with what He wants me to do.

As I write this message, I am thankful to be blessed by God to understand His words and every day I do my best to remain acceptable in his sight.

In closing, I want to leave with 2 Peter 1:2-8, which says, "Grace and peace be multiplied unto you through the knowledge of God, and of Jesus our Lord, according as his divine power has given unto us all things that pertain unto life and godliness, through the knowledge of him that has called us to glory and virtue: Whereby are given unto us exceeding great and precious promises: that by these you might be partakers of the divine nature, having escaped the corruption that is in the world through lust. And besides this, giving all diligence, add to your faith virtue; and to virtue add knowledge; and to knowledge temperance; and to temperance patience; and to patience godliness; and to godliness brotherly kindness; and to brotherly kindness, charity. For if these things be in you, and abound, they make you that you shall neither be barren nor unfruitful in the knowledge of our Lord Jesus Christ."

Have Faith

As I fight this battle, I realize I'm in a serious war. No matter how hard I fight back, my enemy fights back even more. This is a fight about life and death, and it deals with love, health, and wealth. It's about new beginnings and some sad endings with some involving close loved ones and some the loss of dear friends. For as long as I can remember, I've been fighting this fight, and sacrificing everything while pursuing Gods scintillating light.

Yes, this war is about evil versus good and acknowledging the cross Jesus died on was more than a piece of wood. The cross represents the death of sin, and through Jesus puts us back with God spiritually again; Jesus paid the ultimate price. So even when we die physically, we can still have eternal life, which is why I refuse to give up on this fight, not because I don't want to, but because it wouldn't be right.

Sometimes I feel like giving up when it seems it's no win in sight, but that's when my faith carries me on to fight back.

With this I press on, leaning on my faith that is not only mighty but also strong. I am determined I will not fall to defeat. I know my adversary too well. In truth, it's myself I'm trying to beat.

Every one of us will have to face this battle from within. The good part about it is Jesus will fight with us until the end. So fight the good fight and keep moving on, believing Jesus is sitting on the right-hand side of God on his majestic throne. With all his Father's work being finished and done, God subjected all things unto Him, His only begotten Son.

In knowing this, have faith and be still, understanding this is not only our fate, it is our Father's will!

The Bible Is a Map

"**F**or we have not followed cunningly devised fables, when we made known unto you the power and coming of our Lord Jesus Christ, but were eyewitnesses of his majesty. For he received from God the Father honour and glory, when there came such a voice to him from the excellent glory, this is my beloved Son, in whom I am well pleased. And this voice which came from heaven we heard, when we were with him in the holy mount. We have also a more sure word of prophecy; whereunto you do well that you take heed, as unto a light that shines in a dark place, until the day of dawn, and the day star arise in your hearts: Knowing this first: that no prophecy of the scriptures is of any private interpretation. For the prophecy came not in old time by the will of man: but holy men of God spoke as they were moved by the Holy Ghost." 2 Peter 1:16-21.

The Bible is indeed a map and can be used to guide us through any situation based on experiences of the writers of the Scriptures. Everything from marriage to neighbors, how to pray, being tested, patience, karma, and hope are in the Bible. When I use the term of the Bible being a map, it's because the same way we use maps to get from place to place, we can use the Bible to show us the way to eternal life.

The first thing I want to point out is about how to pray. Matthew 6:5-13 says, "And when you pray, you shall not be as the hypocrites are: for the love to pray standing in the synagogues and in the corners of the streets, that they may be seen of men. Verily I say unto you, they have their reward. But you, when you pray, enter unto your closet, and when you have shut your door, pray to your Father which is in secret; and your Father which sees in secret shall reward you openly. But when you pray, use not vain repetitions, as the heathens do: for they think that they shall be heard for their much speaking. Be not you therefore like unto them: for your Father knows the things you have need of, before you ask of him. After this manner therefore pray you: Our Father which art in heaven, Hallowed be your name. Your kingdom come. Your will be done in earth, as it is in heaven. Give us this day our daily bread. And forgive us our debts, as we forgive our debtors. And lead us not into temptation, but deliver us from evil: For thine is the kingdom, and the power, and the glory forever. Amen."

It's important to understand this Scripture and the message in it. First, it lets us know that God knows what we need before we even ask for it, and it tells us how and what to pray for. When I first read Matthew speaking about praying, it changed

my whole outlook about praying because I would do exactly what the Scriptures say don't do like praying the same thing over and over for a long period. Once I learned how to pray, I had to lean on my faith; that was all I needed, and God would take care of all my needs.

When we are troubled by the loss of a loved one or even because someone we love has hurt us, we deal with it in different ways. Some hold things in, some act out, and some simply cry. The Bible shows us that Jesus felt some of the same things we feel. This is why I say the Bible is a map. Everything we go through can be found in the Bible where someone went through the same things.

John 11:32-36 says, "Then when Mary was come where Jesus was, and saw him, she fell down at his feet, saying unto him, Lord, if you had been here, my brother would not have died. When Jesus therefore saw her weeping, and the Jews also weeping which came with her, he groaned in the spirit, and was troubled, And said, Where have you laid him? They said unto him, Lord come and see. Jesus wept. Then said the Jews, Behold how he loved him!"

The whole point in Jesus coming here as a man was to be an example and go through the things we do to show us that if we follow his example, we can be guided back to God, His Father.

Sometimes I felt like I was going through way more than what other people were going through. I would find myself asking God to have mercy on me because I could not take any more hurt or pain from different things and people. But when I read what Paul says in 1 Corinthians 10:13, I knew what I was going through was not something only I was experiencing. Verse 13 says, "There has no temptation taken you but such as is common to man: but God is faithful, who will not suffer you to be tempted above that you are able; but will with the temptation also make a way to escape, that you may be able to bear it." This Scripture is where the old saying, "God will not put more on you than you can bear," comes from.

Some people may question why God tests our faith. I think I can answer that question by saying God is not testing us for Him; it is for our own assurance that we can trust Him. We do it all the time with people we are involved in relationships with to see if we can trust them. So why would we not expect the same to happen in our relationship with God?

The Bible also speaks about reaping what we sow. If we want roses to grow, don't plant thorns. If we want apples to grow, don't plant oranges. Likewise, if we want good to come to us, then do good and be good while doing it!

Galatians 6:7-10 says, "Be not mocked: for whatsoever a man soweth, that shall he also reap. For he that soweth to his flesh shall of the flesh reap corruption; but he that soweth to the Spirit shall of the spirit reap life everlasting. And let us not be weary of well doing: for in due season we shall reap, if we faint not. As we have therefore opportunity, let us do good unto all men, especially unto them who are of the household of faith."

The Scriptures are quite helpful when it comes to following the spirit rather than lusts of the flesh. Galatians5:16-25 says, "This I say then, walk in the spirit, and you shall not fulfill the lusts of the flesh. For the flesh lusteth against the spirit, and the spirit against the flesh: and these are contrary the one to the other: so that you cannot do the things that you would. But if you be led of the Spirit, you are not under the law. Now the works of the flesh are manifest which are these; Adultery, fornications, uncleanness, lasciviousness, idolatry, witchcraft, hatred, variance, emulations, wrath, strife, seditions, heresies, envying, murders, drunkenness, revellings, and such like: of the which I tell you before, as I have also told you in time past, that they which do such things shall not inherit the kingdom of God. But the fruit of the spirit is love, joy, peace, longsuffering, gentleness, goodness, faith, meekness, temperance: against such there is no law. And they that are Christ's have crucified the flesh with the affections and lusts. If we live in the spirit, let us also walk in the spirit."

Ephesians 4:13-32 further instructs us on the paths we should take and the conversations we should have. Verse 13 starts by saying, "Till we all come in the unity of the faith, and of the knowledge of the son of God, unto a perfect man, unto the measure of the stature of the fulness of Christ: That we henceforth be no more children, tossed to and fro, and carried about with every wind of doctrine, by the sleight of men, and cunning craftiness, whereby they lie in wait to deceive; But speaking the truth in love, may grow up into him in all things which is the head, even Christ: From who the whole body fitly joined together and compacted by that which every joint supplieth, according to the effectual working in the measure of every body part, makes increase of the body unto the edifying of itself in love. This I say, therefore, and testify in the Lord, that you henceforth walk not as the other Gentiles walk, in the vanity of their mind, Having the understanding darkened, being alienated from the life of God through the ignorance that is in them, because of the blindness of their heart: who being past feeling have given themselves over unto lasciviousness, to work all uncleanness with greediness. But you have not so learned Christ; If so be that you have heard him, and have been taught by him, as the truth is in Jesus: That you put off concerning the former conversation the old man, which is corrupt according to the deceitful lusts; And be renewed in the spirit of your mind; And that you out on the new man, which after God is created in righteousness and true holiness. Wherefore putting away lying, speak every man truth with his neighbor: for we are members of one another. Be you angry, and sin not: let not the sun go down upon your wrath: Neither give place to the devil. Let him that stole steal no more: but rather let him labor, working with his hands the thing which is good, that he may have to give to him that needs. Let no corrupt communication proceed out of your mouth, but that which is good to the use of edifying that it may minister grace unto the hearers. And grieve not the Holy Spirit of God, whereby you are sealed unto the day of redemption. Let all bitterness, and wrath and anger, and clamor and evil speaking, be put away from you, with all malice: And be kind to one another, tenderhearted, forgiving one another, even as God for Christ sake has forgiven you."

When it comes to people questioning your faith and what the Scriptures say, remember what Titus 3:9 says, "But avoid foolish questions, and genealogies, and contentions, and strivings about the law; for they are unprofitable and vain."

1 Peter4:7-13 tells us to be sober and watch unto prayer and to rejoice. Verse 7 starts by saying, "But the end of all things is at hand: be you therefore sober, and watch unto prayer. And above all things have fervent charity among yourselves: for charity shall cover a multitude of sins. Use hospitality one to another without grudging. As every man has received the gift, even so, minister the same one to another, as good stewards of the manifold grace of God. If any man speaks, let him speak as the oracles of God; if any man minister, let him do it as of the ability which God giveth: that God in things may be glorified through Jesus Christ, to whom be praise and dominion for ever and ever. Amen. Beloved, think it not strange concerning the fiery trial which is to try you, as though some strange thing happened unto you: But

rejoice, inasmuch as you are partakers of Christ's sufferings; that, when his glory shall be revealed, you may be glad also with exceeding joy."

Before I close, I want to direct attention to Hebrews 12:1-11, which says, "Wherefore seeing we are also compassed about with so great a cloud of witnesses, let us lay aside every weight, and the sin which do so easily beset us, and let us run with patience the race that is set before us, looking unto Jesus the author and finisher of our faith; who for the joy that was set before him endured the cross, despising the shame, and is set down at the right hand of the throne of God. For consider him that endured such contradiction of sinners against himself, lest you be wearied and faint in your minds. You have not yet resisted unto blood, striving against sin. And you have forgotten the exhortation which speaks unto you as children, My son, despise not the chastening of the Lord, nor faint when you are rebuked of him: For whom the Lord loves he chastens, and scourgeth every son who he receives. If you endure chastening, God deals with you as with sons; for what son is he who the father chastens not? But if you be without chastisement whereof all are partakers, then you are bastards and not sons, Furthermore we have had fathers of our flesh which corrected us, and we gave them reverence: shall we not much rather be in subjection unto the Father of spirits, and live? For they verily for a few days chastened us after their own pleasure; but he for our profit, that we might be partakers of his holiness. Now no chastening for the present seems to be joyous, but grievous: nevertheless afterward it yields the peaceable fruit of righteousness unto them which are exercised thereby."

All of the verses I've put in this chapter are only the tip of the iceberg. As I stated at the beginning of this chapter, the Bible is a map. Regardless of what we may be going through, we can find an example of how to get over it, under it, through it, or around it. I challenge you to apply the Bible to anything in your life to see if there is an example of it in there, no matter what the subject.

In closing, I want to leave you with a message from Paul out of the book of Philippians 4:8-9, which says, "Finally, brethren, whatsoever things are true, whatsoever things are honest, whatsoever things are just, whatsoever things are pure, whatsoever things are lovely, whatsoever things are of good report; if there be any virtue, and if there be any praise, think on these things. Those things, which you have both learned, and received, and heard, and seen in me, do: and the God of peace shall be with you."

One Day at A Time

Lord, please, help me to live my life one day at a time. Please, Lord, help me to understand Your will so that I will put it before mine. I think I can say I have done all that I wanted to do. Now, Lord, my only desire is to please You. I promise You if You show me Your way, I will follow you forever, even until my last day. How beautiful it is to know Your love for me is never ending and true. I believe You are the creator of heaven, earth, and me, too. Please, help me to raise my kids to know You are real. I want them to know they can come to You, no matter how they feel. I know they were Yours before they were mine. I have faith You will reveal Yourself to them when it is time. Bless me, Father, and forgive me of my sins. I know better now. I promise to do my best and never do them again. I will give you my all until I get it right; I will give You my heart, mind, soul, and love You with all my might. Please, keep me strong and in Your light. Help me, Lord, resist temptation and strengthen me to fight back. Without You, I cannot do anything, but with You, all things are possible, my Lord, my Savior, and my King. Please, Lord, hear this prayer and remember Your promise that You will never forsake me and You will always be there. One day at a time is my prayer to You. I love You, my Lord. Thank You for loving me, too.

CHAPTER 9

Absolute

I s a man a leader or a follower, or could he be one who knows it may be a time to do both? Is a man loud or silent, or is he one who can whisper and be heard by those near and far? Is a man one who goes fast or moves slow, or does a man believe it's not how fast or slow he goes but rather how far he gets? Is a man rough or gentle, or is he capable of conflicts and comforting? Is a man an instigator of war, or does a man initiate peace, or will he know when one is inevitable and deal with it accordingly? Does being a man mean being a good husband to his wife, believing the old adage that behind every good man there is a good woman? Or does a man know that his wife's place is not behind him but beside him? Does being a man mean to be simply a father to his kids, or does a man believe that in being a great father, his number one goal is to guide his children to our Father in heaven. Knowing they were Gods before they became his? Does a man believe in God, or does a man feel he is his own alpha and omega? Does a man feel he lives by chance, but he chooses who and what he loves so he can determine his own destiny? What things are important to a man? Is it love, life, health, and wealth? Or is it merely having peace of mind, financial stability, and a virtuous woman? Can a man ever be satisfied, or will the more he gets, the more he will want? Can a man be defined by any of these things, or is what makes a man his own definition of himself? What makes you a man?

"When I was a child, I spoke as a child, I understood as a child, I thought as a child: but when I became a man, I put away childish things." 1 Corinthians 13:11

Absolute! Absolute is the point I have finally reached after years of going back and forth with believing and doubting. One day, I was meditating in the spirit. It led me to look back on my life and the many trials I had faced and how I emerged on the other side of them. It was precisely at that moment I realized my Lord had been with me throughout my life and all of its ups and downs.

The word absolute sprung from my heart and proceeded out of my mouth. Now I define my faith in God as being unwavering, without question and absolute.

One Scripture, in particular, came to mind when I had this epiphany. It's Romans 8:37-39, where Paul says, "Nay, in all these things we are more than conquerors through him that loved us. For I am persuaded, that neither death, nor life, nor angels, nor principalities, nor powers, nor things present, nor things to come, nor height, nor depth, nor any other creature, shall be able to separate us from the love of God, which is in Christ Jesus our Lord."

That Scripture is so powerful and covers everything to me. I want it to be understood; I have not just read the Bible and hoped that I was doing right, I have sought after God for at least thirty years. The reason I've done this is because I truly love God with all my heart, mind, and soul. Nothing under the sun can fool me into believing there's something more important for me than to live my life the way my Lord has instructed me to do. This is a choice I have made. This book is a testimony that I can't stop and won't stop doing God's will in my life!

Now I want to confess that getting to this point where I'm at today did not come easy for me. It was as if the closer I tried to get, the further God would go away. But just like I've said in this book repeatedly, there is an example in the Bible for everything we go through to help us get past it. Even at some of my lowest points, I learned to take it in stride, and I did with the help of Philippians 3:7-15, which says, "But what things were gain to me, those I counted loss for Christ. Yes doubtless, and I count all things but loss for the excellency of the knowledge of Christ Jesus my Lord: for whom I have suffered the loss of all things, and do count them but dung, that I may win Christ. And be found in him not having my own righteousness, which is the law, but that which is through the faith of Christ, the righteousness which is of God by faith: That I may know him, and the power of his resurrection and the fellowship of his suffering, being made conformable unto his death; If by any means I might attain unto the resurrection of the dead. Not as though I had already attained, either were already perfect: but I follow after, if that I may apprehend that for which also I am apprehended of Christ Jesus. Brothers, I count not myself to have apprehended: but this one thing I do, forgetting those things which are behind, and reaching forth unto those things which are before. I press toward the mark for the prize of the high calling of God in Christ Jesus. Let us therefore, as many as be perfect, be thus minded: and if in any thing you be otherwise minded, God shall reveal even this unto you."

That Scripture may remind us of the story of the man in the chapter on "Riches," who asked Jesus what would it take to inherit the kingdom of heaven. To which Jesus replied, "Sell all that you have and distribute unto the poor and you will have treasure in heaven."

Another Scripture that's important to me having stability in my faith comes from the book of Proverbs. To understand this Scripture is to understand God's words when he says that our faith will be tried and tested. This Scripture also reminds me of the poem called "Footprints." There were many times I begged God to stop my suffering, and in some of those times, I felt like God had left me alone. But now, through faith and experience, I realize that's when God can show us his strength—when we are at our weakest point. \

Proverbs 20:24 says, "Man's goings are of the Lord; how can a man then understand his own way?" What this means is that God already has a plan for our lives. When we set out to follow our own wants is when we suffer because things don't go the way we want. To get to heaven, we must be obedient to God's commandments. To do this, we are limited in the things we can do without going outside of His will.

Matthew 7:13-14 tells us the paths we need to stay on to stay right. Verse 13 starts by saying, "Enter you at the straight gate: for wide is the gate, and broad is the way, that leads to destruction, and many there be which go in thereat: Because straight is the gate, and narrow is the way, which leads unto life, and few there be that find it."

It's important to take heed to this Scripture and not take for granted you will get a free pass to heaven because you called on the name of God, but didn't do His will. Matthew 7:21-22 says, "Not everyone who says unto me, Lord, Lord, shall enter into the kingdom of heaven."

The book of Ecclesiastes tells us there's a time for everything. From this Scripture, I knew it was time for me to give my love and life to my Lord. Even though the Scriptures say that it's a time for everything, does that mean we have time for everything? I realized I could not say, "Well, let me get the things I want and do what I want to do first. Then I will give my life to God."

Matthew 6:24-33 is a great example of why we should not do that. Verse 24 starts by saying, "No man can serve two masters: for either he will hate the one, and love the other; or else he will hold to the one, and despise the other. You cannot serve God and mammon. Therefore I say unto you, Take no thought for your life, what you shall eat, or what you shall drink; nor yet for your body, what you shall put on. Is not the life more than meat and the body more than raiment? Behold the birds of the air: for they sow not, neither do they reap, nor gather into barns; yet your heavenly Father feeds them. Are you much better than them? Which of you by taking thought can add one cubit unto his stature? And why take your thought for raiment? Consider the lilies of the field, how they grow; they toil not, neither do they spin: And yet I say unto you, That even Solomon in all his glory was not arrayed like one of these. Wherefore, if God so clothed the grass of the field, which today is and tomorrow is cast into the oven, shall he not much more clothe you, O you of little faith? Therefore take no thought, saying, What shall we eat? or What shall we drink? or Wherewithal shall we be clothed? (For after all these things do the Gentiles seek:) for your heavenly Father knows that you have need of all these things. But seek you first the kingdom of God, and his righteousness; and all these things shall be added unto you."

I don't think that Scripture can be made any clearer. Not only in that Scripture, but throughout the Bible, God instructs us to seek Him and His will. David says in Psalms 27:8: "When you said, Seek you my face; my heart said unto thee, your face, Lord, will I seek."

I must say it is a beautiful thing to be in line with God. It's not like having a friend to get along with, and really, it's not like having a relationship with someone we love and have fun with. Having a relationship with God cannot be compared to anything we can think of! This is the position I have taken regardless of sunny days or rain. Proverbs 24:10 says, "If you faint in the day of adversity, your strength is small."

The most important thing we must do to accept God is to believe He is real, and there is only one God! Isaiah says, in 45:5: "I am the Lord, and there is none else, there is no God beside me: I girded thee, though you have not known me." James 2:19 goes along with this. Verse 19 says, "You believe that there is one God; you do well: the devils also believe and tremble."

Before I close this chapter, I want to point out three more Scriptures. The first is 1 Corinthians 2:1-16, which says, "And I, brethren, when I came to you, came not with excellency of speech or of wisdom, declaring unto you the testimony of God. For I determined not to know anything among you, save Jesus Christ, and him crucified and I was with you in weakness, and in fear, and in much trembling. And my speech and preaching was not with enticing words of man's wisdom, but in demonstration of the spirit and of power: That your faith should not stand in the wisdom of men, but in the power of God. Howbeit we speak wisdom among them that are perfect: yet not the wisdom of this world, nor of the princes of this world that come to nothing: But we speak wisdom of God in a mystery, even the hidden wisdom, which God ordained before the world unto our glory: Which none of the princes of this world knew: for had they known it, they would not have crucified the Lord of glory. But as it is written, Eye has not seen, nor ear heard, neither have entered into the heart of man, the things which God has prepared for them that love him. But God has revealed them unto us by his spirit: for the spirit searches all things, yes, the deep things of God. For what man knows the things of a man, save the spirit of man which is in him? Even so the things of God knows no man, but the spirit of God. Now we have received, not the spirit of the world, but the spirit which is of God; that we might know the things that are freely given to us of God. Which things also we speak, not in the words which man's wisdom teaches, but which the Holy Ghost teaches; comparing spiritual things with spiritual. But the natural man receives not the things of the spirit of God: for they are foolishness unto him: neither can he know them, because they are spiritually discerned. But he that is spiritual judges all things, yet he himself is judged of no man. For who has known the mind of the Lord, that he may instruct him? But we have the mind of Christ."

I hope this Scripture will let you know I'm not telling you things I think, but rather the words of God. In closing, I will leave you with 2 Corinthians 13:11 which says, "Finally, brethren, farewell. Be perfect, be of good comfort, be of one mind, live in peace; and the God of love and peace will be with you."

"If I have told you of earthly things, and you believe not, how will you believe if I tell you of heavenly things?" John 3:12

CHAPTER 10

Open Chapter

---◆---

"These words spoke Jesus, and lifted up his eyes to heaven, and said Father, the hour is come; glorify thy son: As you have given him power over all flesh, that he should give eternal life to as many as you have given him. And this is life eternal, that they might know you the only true God, and Jesus Christ, who you have sent. I have glorified you on earth: I have finished the work which you gave me to do. And now, O Father, glorify you me with your own self with the glory which I had with you before the world was. I have manifested your name unto men which you gave me out of the world: yours they were, and you gave them to me; and they have kept your word. Now they have known that all things whatsoever you have given me are of you. For I have given unto them the words which you gave me; and they have received them and have known surely that I came out from you, and they have believed that you did send me. I pray not for the world, but for them which you have given me; for they are yours. And all mine are yours and yours mine; and I am glorified in them. And now

I am no more in the world, and I came to you. Holy Father, keep through your own name those who you have given me, that they may be one, as we are. While I was with them in the world, I kept them in your name: those that you gave me I have kept, and none of them is lost, but the son of perdition; that the scripture might be fulfilled. And now come I to you; and these things I speak in the world, that they might have my joy fulfilled in themselves. I have given them your word; and the world has hated them, because they are not of the world even as I am not of the world. I pray not that you should take them out of the world, but that you should keep them from the evil. They are not of the world, even as I am not of the world. Sanctify them through your truth: Your word is truth. As you have sent me into the world, even so I have also sent them into the world. And for their sakes, I sanctify myself, that they also might be sanctified through the truth. Neither pray I for these alone, but for them also which shall believe on me through their word; That they all may be one; as you Father, are in me, and I in you, that they also may be one in us: that the world may believe that you have sent me. And the glory which you gave me I have given them; that they may be one, even as we are one: I in them, and you in me, that they may be made perfect in one; and that the world may know that you have sent me, and have loved them, as you have loved me. Father I will that they also who you have given me, be with me where I am; that they may behold my glory, which you have given me: for you loved me before the foundation of the world. O righteous Father, the world has not known you: but I have known you, and these have known that you have sent me. And I have declared unto them your name, and will declare it: that the love wherewith you have loved me may be in them, and I in them." John 17:1-26

I started this chapter with Jesus praying to his Father, God, about us and for us. Here, we can see how much Jesus loves us by the way He is asking God to accept us. I thought it would be good to have an open chapter to be able to touch on as many topics as possible. This chapter includes a multitude of things that apply to our everyday lives and how the saints were able to deal with them.

When I say saints or prophets and mention their messages as I included in a previous chapter in the Bible, let's be clear that their words were inspired by God and not simply their own account of things. In 2 Peter 1 16-21, he clarifies this by saying, "For we have not followed cunningly devised fables, when we made known unto you the power and coming of our Lord Jesus Christ, but were eyewitnesses of his majesty. For he received from God the Father honour and glory when there came such a voice to him from the excellent glory, this is my beloved son, in who I am well pleased. And this voice which came from heaven we heard, when we were with him in the holy mount. We have also a more sure word of prophecy; whereunto you do well that you take heed, as unto a light that shines in a dark place, until the day dawn, and the day star arise in your hearts:

knowing this first, that no prophecy of the scripture is of any private interpretation. For the prophecy came not in old time by the will of man: but holy men of God spoke as they were moved by the Holy Ghost."

It's important to mention that the writers of the Bible were moved by the Holy Ghost to say the things they did.

The Bible says that all manners of sin committed by men can be forgiven but one. Regardless of what we have heard about some sin being unforgiven by God, Matthew 12:31-32 clears this up when he says, "Therefore I say unto you, all manner of sin and blasphemy shall be forgiven unto men: but the blasphemy against the Holy Ghost shall not be forgiven unto men. And whosoever speaks a word against the Son of man, it shall be forgiven him: but whosoever speaks against the Holy Ghost, it shall not be forgiven him, neither in this world, neither in the world to come." This does not mean that we can go on committing sins thinking we have a free pass. It just means our Lord is so full of mercy that He will forgive our sins as long as we press toward His mark.

When I think about forgiveness, a Scripture comes to mind that lets us know we will all face judgment, believer and non-believers. It is 1 Peter 4:17, which says, "For the time is come that judgment must begin at the house of God: and if it first begins at us, what shall the end be of them that obey not the gospel of God?"

This Scripture makes it clear that just because we say we believe and have faith doesn't mean we won't face judgment. The verse says judgment will begin at the house of God first. In knowing we can be forgiven for all but one sin, we should be willing to confess them and ask for forgiveness rather than thinking God won't hold us accountable for them.

Proverbs 28:13 says, "He that covers his sins shall not prosper: but whoso confesses and forsake them shall have mercy." If all we have to do is confess our sins to God to be forgiven, why would we not do it? If we don't, we will be faced with the punishment for sin. Romans 6:23 says, "For the wages of sin is death, but the gift of God is eternal life through Jesus Christ our Lord."

To get forgiveness, we must admit our sins; then through God's mercy, we can be cleansed. Proverbs 16:6-7 says, "By mercy and truth iniquity is purged: and by the fear of the Lord men depart from evil. When a man's ways please the Lord, he makes even his enemies to be at peace with him."

Everything goes back to faith. I say again that our whole religion is based on faith, which is extremely powerful if we truly have unwavering faith.

We must not only have faith, but we must live by it. Romans 1:17 says, For therein is the righteousness of God revealed from faith to faith: as it is written, The just shall live by faith." Hebrews 11:16 tells us that without faith, it is impossible to please him: for he that comes to God must believe that he is, and that he is a rewarder of them that diligently seek him.

In the book of Joshua, there is Scripture that tells us how we can establish faith that will sustain us through whatever we encounter. At the same time, it tells us our Lord will be with us at all times. Joshua 1:8-9 says, "This book of the law shall not depart out of your mouth; but you shall meditate therein day and night, that you may observe to do according to all that is written therein: for then you shall make your way prosperous, and then you shall have good success. Have I not commanded you? Be strong and of good courage; be not afraid, neither be you dismayed: for the Lord your God is with you wherever you go."

If we take Joshua's advice, then follow them with Paul's words in 2 Corinthians 10:5, things will become clearer for us to understand. Paul says, "Casting down imaginations, and every high thing that exalts itself against the knowledge of God, and bringing into captivity every thought to the obedience of Christ."

When I first read that Scripture, it became clear I was having thoughts that were against the word of God such as revenge, judging others, and questions about the Bible I did not know the answers to. Again, the Scriptures made all the answers clear. About vengeance, Romans 12:19 says, "Dearly beloved, avenge not yourselves, but rather give place to wrath: for it is written, Vengeance is mine; I will repay saith the Lord."

About judging others, Romans 2:1-3 says, "Therefore you are inexcusable, O man, whosoever you are that judge: for wherein you judge another, you condemn yourself; for you that judges do the same things. But we are sure that the judgment of God is according to truth against them which commit such things. And think you this, O man, that judges them which do such things, and do the same, that you shall escape the judgment of God?"

About questions that I did not know the answers to, Titus 3:8 says, "But avoid foolish question sand genealogies, and contentions, and strivings about the law; for they are unprofitable and vain."

I only listed three things; however, as I've said from the beginning of this book, everything we can think of is in the Bible. No matter what we're going through, we can use the Bible as a map to guide us past it. There is an important story in the Scriptures about people judging others. I want to mention judging again because it's a key component to not being judged.

John 8: 1-11 says, "Jesus went into the Mount of Olives. And early in the morning he came again into the temple, and all the people came unto him; and he sat down, and taught them. And the Scribes and Pharisees brought unto him a woman taken in adultery, in the very act. Now Moses in the law commanded us, that such should be stoned: but what say you? This they said, tempting him that they might have to accuse him. But Jesus stooped down, and with his finger wrote on the ground, as though he heard them not. So when they continued asking him, he lifted up himself and said unto them, He that is without sin among you, let him first cast a stone at her. And again he stooped down, and wrote on the ground. And they which heard it, being convicted by their own conscience went out one by one, beginning at the eldest, even unto the last: and Jesus was left alone, and the woman standing in the midst. When Jesus had lifted up himself, and saw none but the woman, he said unto her, Woman where are those your accusers? Have no man condemned you? She said, no man, Lord. And Jesus said unto her, Neither do I condemn you: go, and sin no more."

Can you imagine the thought of being in the presence of Jesus while He was on earth? Even with all that He did, people still did not believe. Yes, there were some who did believe, but there were more who did not than did. I would do anything to have been in those times and been blessed to walk and talk to Jesus. As I write this book, I realize that I'm still learning. But it's love in motion to me.

As I progress, I understand I have to be careful and mindful of the things I say. James

3:10 says, "Out of the same mouth proceeds blessings and cursing. My brethren, these things ought not so to be."

The Scriptures even tells us that it's not what goes into a man that defiles him, but rather what comes out of him. Mark 7:18-23 says, "And he said unto them, Are you so without understanding also? Do you not perceive, that whatsoever thing from without enters into the man, it cannot defile him; Because it enters not into his heart, but into the belly, and goes out into the draught, purging all meats? And he said, That which comes out of the man that defiles the man. For from within, out of the heart of men proceed evil thoughts, adulteries, fornications, murders, thefts, covetousness, wickedness, deceit, lasciviousness, an evil eye, blasphemy, pride, foolishness: All these evil things come from within, and defile the man."

Another reason we have to control what goes in and out of our bodies is because our bodies are the temples where we dwell. 1 Corinthians 3:16-17 says, "Know you not that you are the temple of God, and that the Spirit of God dwells in you? If any man defiles the temple of God, him shall God destroy; for the temple of God is holy, which temple you are."

Once I became convinced the Bible is truly God's words, I took on a different set of values shaped by Paul in the book of Philippians 4:11-13, which says, "Not that I speak in respect of want: for I have learned, in whatsoever state I am, therewith to be content. I know both how to be abased, and I know how to abound: everywhere and in all things, I am instructed both to be full and to be hungry, both to abound and to suffer need. I can do all things through Christ which strengthens me."

It could be easy for some to assume that because things are not going the way they want them to go, they are not blessed. But Matthew 5:3-12 lets us know that those who may be struggling are still blessed. Verse begins by saying, "Blessed are the poor in spirit: for theirs is the kingdom of heaven. Blessed are they that mourn: for they shall be comforted. Blessed are the meek: for thy shall inherit the earth. Blessed are they who hunger and thirst after righteousness for they shall be filled. Blessed are the merciful: for they shall obtain mercy: Blessed are the pure in heart: for they shall see God. Blessed are the peacemakers: for they shall be called the children of God. Blessed are they which are persecuted for righteousness sake: for theirs is the kingdom of heaven. Blessed are you, when men shall revile you, and persecute you, and shall say all manner of evil against you falsely, for my sake. Rejoice, and be exceedingly glad: for great is your reward in heaven: for so persecuted they the prophets which were before you."

When we think of blessings from God, we must be thankful for the things seen and unseen. We can learn this from 2 Corinthians 4:18, which says, "While we look not at the things which are seen, but at the things which are not seen: for the things which are seen are temporal; but the things which are not seen are eternal."

As I wind this chapter down, I want to go back and remind you not to sleep on Satan and his tricks. I know I wrote the chapter "From a Serpent to a Dragon" and how he was called

Satan, Lucifer, and even the devil, but in Isaiah 14:12-17, he is also called a man. Verse 12 starts with saying, "How art you fallen from heaven, O Lucifer, son of the morning! How art you cut down to the ground, which did weaken the nations! For you have said in your heart, I will ascend into heaven, I will exalt my throne above the stars of God: I will sit also upon the mount of the congregation, in the sides of the north: I will ascend above the heights of the clouds; I will be like the Most High. Yet you shall be brought down to hell, to the sides of the pit. They that see you shall narrowly look upon you, and consider you saying, Is this the man that made the earth tremble, that did shake the kingdoms: That made the world as a wilderness, and destroyed the cities thereof; that opened not the house of his prisoners?"

I included this verse to show that Satan not only hates us, but he hates God as well, and wants to become God rather than submit to Him. One of Satan's oldest tricks is the division of races. Prejudice in simple terms. I say to you, don't be deceived, trust in God, have faith, have mercy and forgiveness, have peace and above all have love!

I will close this book with the last message Jesus gives to us, and it is in the last chapter of the Bible, Revelation 22:16-21, which says, "I, Jesus, have sent my angels to testify unto you these things in the churches. I am the root and the offspring of David, and the bright and morning star. And the spirit of the bride says, Come! And let him that hear say, Come! And let him that is athirst come. And whosoever will, let him take the water of life freely. For I testify unto every man that hears the words of the prophecy of this book, If any man shall take away from the words of the book of this prophecy. God shall take away his part out the Book of Life, and out of the holy city, and from the things which are written in this book. He which testify these things says, Surely I come quickly. Amen. Even so, come, Lord Jesus. The grace of our Lord Jesus Christ be with you all. Amen." Be clear the book spoken of in that Scripture is indeed the Bible.

One God, one mind, one love, and one action! Praise God! It is finished, my Lord.

A New Beginning

Each day is not merely a new day; it's also a new beginning to strive toward fulfilling our goals. Each new day presents the chance for us to refine and define ourselves. It gives us the chance to grow beyond measure and evolve into our visions. Each new beginning gives us the confidence to know that we live by chance, but we love by choice so that we can determine our own destiny. We know we can be the sunrise and sunset of each day by scintillating from within. Using our own light to illuminate the paths we create as we go forward.

With each new beginning, we should entwine with the opportunity the desire to give our best as we trust in God to do the rest. When we reach our apex, it is at that point that we become aware that God is not only the author of our life but also the finisher of our salvation. When we use each new beginning, it is essential that we acknowledge God in all aspects of our love and life as we seek stability in our health and wealth. As we proceed, our push should be toward the truth as we inspire others around us to be witnesses to the truth, that God is our Alpha and Omega. If this is not a point you have reached in your journey through this life, with your new beginning, I encourage you to dig deep within yourself as you continue your voyage to fulfill your destiny, which is to become absolute!

Summary

---◇---

"**M**aster, which is the great commandment in the law? Jesus said unto him, You shall love the Lord your God with all your heart, and with all your soul, and with all your mind. This is the first and great commandment." Matthew 22:36-38

While writing this book, I included at least 130 Scriptures as reference points, so readers can confirm what I wrote was consistent with the Bible. The whole purpose was to touch on subjects that are outstanding to me. Every chapter was based on things I had to overcome.

It is my true hope that the many Scriptures in this book will be researched by you, and in the process, lead you to study the entire Bible.

Making the decision to know God is something we must all come to terms with. This is not a choice of what clothes you will wear, what food you will eat, or who you choose to love. The choice of knowing and accepting God is about heaven and eternal life!

I encourage all of you to be serious about your choices and realize that they will have consequences! In the end, we will all have to give an account of ourselves.

If your end was today and you were to be judged by God on all of your goods vs. bads, rights vs. wrongs, and the outcome being heaven or hell, where would you go? Is your answer based on Scripture, or would it be simply your own belief?

"For it is written, As I live, says the Lord, every knee shall bow to me, and every tongue shall confess to God. So then each of us shall give account of himself to God." Romans 14:11-12

ACKNOWLEDGMENTS

I want to acknowledge my mother, Mrs. Patricia Green, who was instrumental in leading me to the Scriptures and for her years of praying for me and my salvation.

My mother's example of faith was consistent, regardless of sun or rain, happiness or pain. She always believed her Lord was the author and finisher of all things, and it was all about letting His will be done!

Thank you, Mom, my love, for you is eternal. Though we may be separated by space and time, I will see you again based on my belief that we still have one God, one faith, one love, and one mind!

I also want to acknowledge my sister, Mrs. Shelia L. Mack, for truly being her brother's keeper!

www.ingramcontent.com/pod-product-compliance
Lightning Source LLC
Chambersburg PA
CBHW071621040426
42452CB00009B/1430